T0400606

GETTING AROUND IN MY TOWN

TAKING A
FERRY

By Owen Hamlin

Consultant: Beth Gambro
Reading Specialist, Yorkville, Illinois

BEARPORT
PUBLISHING

Minneapolis, Minnesota

Teaching Tips

Before Reading

- Look at the cover of the book. Discuss the picture and the title.

- Ask readers to brainstorm a list of what they already know about taking the ferry. What can they expect to see in the book?

- Go on a picture walk, looking through the pictures to discuss vocabulary and make predictions about the text.

During Reading

- Read for purpose. Encourage readers to think about the kinds of ways they can get around in their town.

- Ask readers to look for the details of the book. What are the steps to taking the ferry?

- If readers encounter an unknown word, ask them to look at the sounds in the word. Then, ask them to look at the rest of the page. Are there any clues to help them understand?

After Reading

- Encourage readers to pick a buddy and reread the book together.

- Ask readers to name two things they might do while taking the ferry. Find the pages that tell about these things.

- Ask readers to write or draw something they learned about taking the ferry.

Credits

Cover and title page, © 22Imagesstudio/Adobe Stock; 3, © NuFa Studio/Adobe Stock; 5, © chameleonseye/iStock; 6–7, © Jim Legault/iStock; 9, © Cheschhh/iStock; 11, © Valeriy_G/iStock; 12, © ColleenMichaels/Adobe Stock; 13, © Jacob Wackerhausen/iStock; 15, © tatyana_tomsickova/iStock; 16–17, © CL Shebley/Shutterstock; 18–19, © DoraDalton/iStock; 21, © Alex Potemkin/iStock; 22, © thailand_becausewecan/Shutterstock, © yilmazsavaskandag/iStock, and © bloodua/iStock; 23TL, © kool99/iStock; 23TM, © Dragoncello/iStock; 23TR, © Bouillante/iStock; 23BL, © MNStudio/iStock; 23BM, © alexsl/iStock; 23BR, © MicroStockHub/iStock.

See BearportPublishing.com for our statement on Generative AI Usage.

Library of Congress Cataloging-in-Publication Data

Names: Hamlin, Owen, 2000- author.
Title: Taking a ferry / by Owen Hamlin.
Description: Minneapolis, Minnesota : Bearport Publishing Company, [2025]
 | Series: Getting around in my town | Includes bibliographical references and index.
Identifiers: LCCN 2024024243 (print) | LCCN 2024024244 (ebook) | ISBN
 9798892326285 (library binding) | ISBN 9798892327084 (paperback) | ISBN
 9798892326681 (ebook)
Subjects: LCSH: Ferries--Juvenile literature.
Classification: LCC HE5751 .H36 2025 (print) | LCC HE5751 (ebook) | DDC
 386/.2234--dc23/eng/20240628
LC record available at https://lccn.loc.gov/2024024243
LC ebook record available at https://lccn.loc.gov/2024024244

For more information, write to Bearport Publishing, 5357 Penn Avenue South, Minneapolis, MN 55419.

Contents

Splash!

Today, we are going into the city.

How will we get there?

Let's take a ferry!

Ferries are big boats that travel across water.

Some ferries carry cars.

People drive right onto the ferry.

Other ferries take only people.

The ferry leaves at certain times each day.

We check the **schedule** on our phone.

That way we know when to get to the ferry.

Say schedule like SKEJ-ool

It is a short walk to the dock.

As we get close, I can see the boat.

It is really big.

We buy **tickets** for the trip.

Soon, it is time to **board** the ferry.

We wait in line to get on the boat.

Let's go to the top **deck**.

From there, we can see all around.

I like looking down at the water.

It is time to leave.

The **captain** drives the boat away from the dock.

We are off!

After a while, we go inside.

People are sitting down on **benches**.

There is a place to get snacks.

Yum!

The boat pulls up to the dock in the city.

The trip is over.

I love taking the ferry!

Parts of a Ferry

A ferry gets us around our town. Let's look at its parts.

Window

Top deck

Captain

Water

Dock

Glossary

benches long seats for two or more people

board to get onto a boat

captain the person who drives a boat

deck a level or floor of a boat

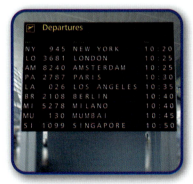

schedule a list of times for when things happen

tickets papers that show a trip has been paid for

Index

Read More

Andrews, Elizabeth.
*Why Does a Boat Float?
(Science Questions).*
Minneapolis: Pop!, 2022.

Anthony, William.
*Boats (Level 4–Blue
Set).* Minneapolis:
Jump!, Inc., 2024.

Learn More Online

1. Go to **FactSurfer.com** or scan the QR code below.
2. Enter "**Taking a Ferry**" into the search box.
3. Click on the cover of this book to see a list of websites.

About the Author

Owen once rode a ferry in Michigan. His
favorite part was the snacks!